THE POEMS OF Christy Brown

BY THE SAME AUTHOR

My Left Foot
Down All the Days

THE POEMS OF Christy Brown

STEIN AND DAY/*Publishers*/New York

First published in 1971
Copyright © 1971 by Christy Brown
Library of Congress Catalog Card No. 78-163350
All rights reserved
Designed by David Miller
Printed in the United States of America
Stein and Day/*Publishers*/7 East 48 Street, New York, N. Y. 10017
ISBN 0-8128-1414-2

CONTENTS

For Ann

For helping to keep the ship afloat

Come Softly to My Wake

Come softly to my wake
on Pavlova feet
at the graying end of day;
into the smoke and heat
enter quietly smiling, quietly unknown
among the garrulous guests
gathered in porter nests
to reminisce and moan;
come not with ornate grief
to desecrate my sleep
but a calm togetherness of hands
quiet as windless sands
and if you must weep
be it for the old quick lust
now lost in dust
only you could shake
from its lair.

Come softly to my wake
and drink and break
the rugged crust
of friendly bread
and weep not for me dead
but lying stupidly there
upon the womanless bed
with a sexless stare
and no thought in my head.

Fog

A lugubrious foghorn in the shrouded distance
scarves of mist swirling up the avenue;
in the gray garden over the way
a red-hulled little boat stood perched
as out of depth as I.
Obscure glints of light in the goldfish bowl
the ancient Alsatian lolling at my feet
fleece technicolored from the carpet dye.
Crunch of wheels on gravel.

I pensively sipped my drink
staring out at the unseen lawn
hearing her quiet movements in the kitchen
preparing lunch for her children
answering their unanswerable questions.

At last briefly alone
we discussed careful, unhurtful things.
The lithograph above the fireplace
surrealist symbol of a wedding feast
an obese satyr keeled over dead drunk
gnomic guests floating eerily in the shadows
hardly in life
hardly delineated.
She knelt to heap more coal on the fire
her face lit by the jealous flames
warmly in life
perfectly delineated.

The old tenderness breeding the old pain
creeping across the whispering room
not to be drowned on any amber sea of burnt brandy.
My trapped senses slid and slithered on ice
hot as the hissing coals.
I stared at a pair of her faded pink slippers
imagined her toes in them
most ordinary and naked
and savagely devoured my drink.

I did not understand the taximan's anger
taking me brutally back
under the haloed lights of the city.
For in all that furious fog
foaming and fuming in from the invisible sea
he had merely lost his way.

Wishful

I would be free of pavements
newspapers of no news
clocks that bully my existence
cars that whisk me away like God
descending unannounced upon me
buses that move as lugubrious elephants
horses fettered to the stupid hands of men.

I am tired to tears of the mental life
of my room full of the ghosts
of never-known things
this spluttering monster machine
creaking into rusty senility
its hammerstrokes deciphering for innocent posterity
my heart's sudden audaciousness.

I would gather about me soft-sandaled things
shadows on a burning lake
trees bending to the earth in love.
Where oh where are the beautiful people?
—the quick of wit
the clowns who spit
in life's sanctimonious countenance
the insolent
the indolent
the fey and gay
with sunlight dripping down their limbs?

I would pawn my hypothetical soul
to wake sudden in the dawn
and find a girl's footprints in dew outside my door.

What Her Absence Means

It means
        no madcap delight will intrude
into the calm flow of my working hours
        no ecstatic errors perplex
my literary pretensions.

It means
        there will be time enough for thought
undistracted by brown peril of eye
        and measured litany of routine deeds
undone by the ghost of a scent.

It means
        my neglect of the Sonnets will cease
and Homer come into battle once more.
        I might even find turgid old Tennyson
less of a dead loss now.

It means
        there will be whole days to spare
for things important to a man—
        like learning to live without a woman
without altogether losing one's mind.

It means
        there is no one now to read my latest poem
with veiled unhurried eyes

putting my nerves on the feline rack
in silence sheer she-devil hell for me.

It means
there is no silly woman to tell me
"Take it easy—life's long anyway—
don't drink too much—get plenty of sleep—"
and other tremendous cliches.

It means
I am less interrupted now with love.

Routine

There is a pattern in sinning
that takes the savor from the act.
Today I could weep for my sins
and tomorrow call myself a fool
yielding to the after-tiredness of indulgence.
There's no use crying over spilt sperm.
What I do and regret today
I'll do and regret tomorrow
and whatever other tomorrow I may see
with undiminished intensity.

Sin on a grand scale wouldn't be so bad.
Three-dimensional
Todd-AO
auditory, visual, aromatic, cinemascopic sin
with a beat and a boom and a bang to it.
Sin biblical as Saul struck blind
and Magdalen's breasts curving over the dawn.
It is the inch-by-wary-inch
antiseptic, deodorized, medically approved
behind-closed-shutters
closed-circuit, do-it-yourself type of sin-making
that sucks a man dry
as a well-sucked orange
trapping the poor wriggling eel-like thoughts
in the wet and ragged net
of his dull iniquities.

A glass of fine brandy renders some solace
and even at today's price
is cheaper than a full confession.

Idyll

Shall we go and lean by the river
in the dusk and peace under the old red bridge
where thoughts fall cool as leaves
beyond the barbed-wire fence of words?

Shall we go out from the city
      the little stone habitats of pin-striped people
      the twilight lovers of much knowledge and little faith;
      the tired time-killers, youth-killers, lady-killers
      making lugubrious love by electric clocks;
      the bottom-kissers of arid ambition,
      the soapbox demagogues of mangled moralities
      with their little household gods
      of security, swivel chairs, position, trim lawns, trim lusts,
      semidetached conjugalities in suburbia,
      their weekend-away-from-home idyll,
      contraceptives secreted in pound-pregnant wallets
      in whose martini mouths love is a sniggered aside
      bandied about from bedroom to bedroom, bosom to bosom
      in dull debauchery of denuded sense . . .
Shall we go lest we become less than magnanimous
      and end by impossibly hating them?

Shall we go and lean by the river
in the dusk and peace under the old red bridge
where the water is clear as the mind never is
and the fishes do not wish to go to the moon?

Poem to Margaret

Child of light
skipping down the eggshell path
of your butterfly years

yellow tendrils
skying wild behind you
swept back by your delight

a flower about to open
about to gladden the world
petal by milky petal

gather me a daisy chain
made from your joy
to wear in my winter

when the glow of now
pales to the far scent
of fragile frost

Margaret of the marigold ways
running across deep October fields
drowning me in the pollen

of your madcap years
making pain seem solace
all child and sudden wisdom

amazing me.

Amour Profane

I shall watch you in the dawn
come slowly awake
slightly bemused by it all
your after-love face
terror gone
hunger slaked
a young girl again
naked and new
that night having lain
not merely with a lover
but love.

We will talk clear words
in the calm after love
catch new worlds
in the shape of each shadow.
Not for us the man-woman prison
of the normal and healthy
the normal and selfish
the slow gnawing of years
the slow bite of cancer
shredding bruised minds.
Scourge of routine
scourge of security
ceremony of love
without celebration
rounding our days to a covenant.
Love is not bound
save by freedom

and love's final word
remains unuttered.
Even we in our slight wisdom
know this.

I shall watch you in the dawn
tumble from sleep
the mist gone
and I content
with the knowledge of you on earth.

One Day and Another

Within the desert of my arms
where you have never lain
I hold the yesterday shadow of you
subtle and gone as smoke.

Within my celibate cell
where late you sat bringing light
I hold your fragile fragrance
safe from the jealous wind.

Into my tomfoolery tumble of words
falling from me as blood
did your heart catch the whisper of a pain
too loud to be heard?

Within my hovel of flesh
you made brief haven of my loss
and I hold your shadow as hostage
past the last dying of my savage hope.

II
NON-ARRIVAL

You did not come.

And as far as I know the world went on
spinning on its merry murderous way
and the clock chimed brutally on
and nothing very disastrous happened.
I even heard people go singing down the street
singing me out of existence.

The face upon my canvas today
is ugly and doomed as hope gone mad
and I envy it its final despair.

Poems run amok in my room
demented denizens of my livid hours
cruelly aborted out of this rage
stinging my senses—as burning flesh
burning at heart's-dead-end of day.

You did not come.
And the whiskey tastes remarkably the same—
my poison now as love was once.

Lines of Leaving

I am losing you again
all again
as if you were ever mine to lose.
The pain is as deep
beyond formal possession
beyond the fierce frivolity of tears.

Absurdly you came into my world
my time-wrecked world
a quiet laugh below the thunder.
Absurdly you leave it now
as always I foreknew you would.
I lived on an alien joy.

Your gentleness disarmed me
wine in my desert
peace across impassable seas
path of light in my jungle.

Now uncatchable as the wind you go
beyond the wind
and there is nothing in my world
save the straw of salvation in the amber dream.
The absurdity of that vast improbable joy.
The absurdity of you gone.

The Hooley

A quick hairtossing turn of head
    and down the narrow aisle of tables you came
        to where I sat a bitter, convivial host
           in a cage of chattering guestbirds
under a sham painting of an absurd youth
    poised girlishly in midstream beneath the Argus bell
        that the happily unenlightened call capital Art.
An hour since I had watched for you
    out into the early streetlamp-lit dusk,
        sternly undrunk in pressed suit and tie
           despite that day's dull debaucheries,
and fumed at your latecoming as at a slowcoach wife;
    left the house in fine fettle of anger,
        and so sat in a corner of crowded desolation
           till with swift hairtossing turn of head
you came, spying me instantly out in the sweat and smoke
        and sat beside me not saying much.

The spray of outflung words fell about me uncaught;
    briefly I sailed out from your haven
        on a porpoise wave of alcohol
           to some fragile shore of peace
a Crusoe in tortured quest of Girl Friday,
    seeking you beyond the bruised moment,
        the breakneck pace of the galloping hours;
           and found only silence huge and coiled
prowling in the undergrowth of panic
    drowning me in its enraged sea-lion's roar.

Somewhere on the humpbacked midnight
in the jam-packed, sardine-tight, rollicking house
I found you in the coolness of the window
—islanded on the sea-lapping fringe
of faces, voices, feet din-drumming
and your eyes were murderously gentle
in their brown sea-foam gaze
as I mouthed my bullying, prison-cell love
and soft without intent
I touched your near, bare arm
in dumb-play of deaf-mute need
from out the harpooned heart of that hour,
and fell back defeated by love,
and sailed far out upon the dim seas of my loss
though I cried to you passionately
all along the dead shore of that dead, dead sea;
somewhere in the depths of that jezebel-ridden night
of bronzed, brazen bewildered uproar I lost you,
and I did not even know.

Windy Interlude

On that ribbon road in the hills
you wool-jacketed against the wind
above the river and the rock-leaping children
we dissected the bones of old hurts
laughed gravely at old fallacies
told ourselves brave unhappy things
in sudden breakaway audacity of heart
I seeing not the uncertain sky
but the ever-changing heaven of your face
my heart glutted on this wonder
you most near
the green freedom around us
the tumult in the peace of that day.

The first slow raindrop touched my cheek;
I did not heed it
peacock-proud by you
this moment never to be betrayed
on this leaden earth.
Your head was bare
leaving your hair to blow in the wind.
Upon your sudden-remote face
a tremendous understanding
as if you knew why the day had turned traitor
and the curlew's cry died even as we heard it.

You did not see me then.
Something deeper held your eye and heart
and made the impetuous word die upon my tongue.

Surf

The wind swept along the deserted promenade
tossing the screeching gulls aloft
as hieroglyphics in the wet smoking air.
Out toward Howth the lighthouse stood
shrouded in the lonely mist. I was glad
nobody was there this scene to share.
The day was brother to my mood.
When sudden below the parapet in the soft
dull sand lay a girl in a red raincoat
and a thin-templed man with sloping shoulders.
He was kissing her throat.

I gazed blindly away to the seething boulders
hearing the sea's deep-bellied chaff;
a little terrier boat heading bravely west
with sails full curved like a woman's breast.
The sky had a snowing look, a serpent glare.
I looked, lacking you beyond that vast opposing flood.
I was near to heart-bursting, near to maniac laugh.
Against the swollen clouds the Bailey stood
a domed red-capped finger at heaven facing.
The gulls wrote asterisks in the air.

Below the crumbling seaweed wall the couple were embracing
dim in the heaping mist, the hooded swirl
of dull-edged foam down the bruised shore,
the man half-shielding the recumbent girl
her hair wild about his obscured face
in a brown tangle. Above the roar

of chaotic nature did I catch a sound
half strangled love, half primal pain?
Long in all that steaming gull-haunted waste
I stared down at the flattened sand where they had lain.

Sunday Morning

They troop by in twos and threes
with covered heads and uncovered knees
scented bright queenly exteriors
matted eyelashes and articulate posteriors.

In possessive suits or flaring dresses
uplifted mounds of lacquered tresses
each Sunday they come their wriggling way
to preen, to gossip, and perhaps to pray.

In garrulous groups or discreet pairs
they blithely bask in rude male stares
while this impious member of the congregation
thinks thoughts of lovely copulation.

No worthy philosophic themes
disturb my holy Sabbath dreams;
for what has Eternity to offer better
than a girl in a tight skirt and sweater?

High Noon

The girl on the beach knows nothing but sun
bearing down on her bare.

What does the large or small future hold;
will the volcano erupt;
are the sharks gathering down in the bay;
what is happening meanwhile back in the jungle;
where have all the young men gone
with all their bright young lusts;
will success spoil Mary Jordan;
is it now the time of year to put fresh flowers
on her mother's ten-year-old grave;
will the Moon of Manakura shine for her;
will the glowworms glow
in the parched brown grasses of the summit
outshining the lights of the scimitar bay;
will her ship of stars sail in one fine day
bearing her starry lover across the seas;
will he have hair on his forearms;
will the lotus bloom for her;
will the herdsman whistle up the eating-dogs
and bake the breadfruit pies;
should she wear nylons in this really tropical weather
                                we're having
for that most pressing engagement tonight at eight
with the manager of the fresh-fruit factory . . . ?

The girl on the beach knows nothing but sun
bearing down on her bare.

In Passing

When you and I were there and all the world,
    joy a berry crushed between our lips,
your breast-lifting arms stretched to the sun,
    standing triumphant, toes square in the sand,
dark wing of hair blowing across your eyes
    and upon us the lovely lassitude of love.

With fingers fast-joined we held the universe in,
    laughing high and free upon the wind,
summer lightning upon our quicksilver tongues
    wild in the days of our needing,
wanton and wild the dark rush of life in us
    hectic in the plunging of our blood.

And you and I were there and all the world.

You are gone, the joy-berry of the world,
    attainment now a hard thing held in the palm,
gone the brilliant foolish talk, the singing vein
    surging to its final frantic victory.
Love now is a clean-cut conception, a logical aftermath,
    solid, stolid as a house,
passion now a covenant, an indulgence, a sophisticated exercise.
    You are here still, new, and yet no longer new,
no longer a challenge, a discovery, an ever-changing sky.
    The you that was within is gone, and so am I.
And we smile and close our eyes and are polite.
    There are no new things in our world now

to dare and bedevil us into splendid flights of folly.

Only placid satisfied faces, trim lawns, bookshelves,
white shirtfronts, punctual cocktails, skies with nothing in them,
blue and vast and empty as those of an idiot.
People who say "thank you" and "do come again soon"
and "that dress you wore to the theater suits you very much"
and—"I *so* enjoyed your letter of the tenth . . ."

Lines Out of Nowhere

You do not appear
nowhere down all the mazed days of my searching
in this autumnal spring of sorrow;

you stepped smiling and sure
out of the walled garden of my heart
into some improbable tomorrow.

My heart knows you still most intimately;
roots run deep in my garden
though I might miss your face in a crowd.

Joy played awhile with my dreams
then gravely gathered them up
in a shroud.

A little time of pleasure
but mine while time is known;
now only this I know—

that wherever you are in time
by whomsoever loved,
my heart will go

still capable of song
though faint and ineffable
as fragrance of frost.

You taught me a thing of much moment;
I did not know one could live
with life itself lost.

Abel

My brother Cain the afflicted likes to sit
brushing softly my shoulder by the water
at night's edge, or in a cinema dimlit
where scenes of peace turn to scenes of slaughter.

Sometimes he will talk to me; his voice
murmurs the commotion in his mind
and begs me to delay my final choice
and I obey, for he is wise and kind.

He shall choose the last long pain for me;
he knows the thing that must be done, my brother;
it is not treachery—our love was free,
it is no will of his or mine, but rather

the timeless tyranny of things ordained
makes life seem death and love reflected hate;
and full my heart, my sacrifice unstained:
"I wait for you, my brother, at the gate."

Meridian

She's not as beautiful as she used to be;
      there's an ageing on her
      the eye might not see
      and the still generous heart might condone;
but the mind, that merciless surveyor,
      will not be appeased by memory
of her former excellences.

The charm of her presence
      grows threadbare thin;
      her letters no longer enchant;
      she's as familiar as a well-worn coat.
It is therefore sobering to reflect
      that one day I too will be forty.

Multum in Parvo

I tell you, she is all you need—
a mascara marvel, a Max Factor de Milo
streamlined and scented, without a blotch
(if you except the falsies and the rubber crotch)
but guaranteed.

Though she struts about brash and bold
in leather jacket and thigh-high boots
and whenever she feels receptive
stubbornly insists on a contraceptive—
she really has a heart of gold.

She's fit and vital and quite willing
to bring you sedatives in bed
and uncan your favorite dish
and copulate whenever you wish
and not demand an extra shilling.

What greater love than this?
She can talk for hours without saying a thing
and your aching muscles rub
as you sit stark in a bathtub;
what greater love than this?

You want *love*? Oh grow up!
That went out with hansom cabs
and who is there to deny
it wasn't all one bloody lie—
a tale told in a teacup?

She has enough to carry her
despite the rubberoid accessories;
no neurosis or complex
believing religiously in sex
and anyhow she is your last resort—marry her!

Inheritance

To the blandished bowl of sky
leaps the insatiable hawk
in spinning spirals of mazed enquiry
seeking the blurred hieroglyphics of its beginning.
Deaf-mute tongues of tongue-tied thoughts
flare across the oceanic wastes of a room
loud as an afternoon landscape
sharp as a knife in the ribs
blade-toothed serpentine whispers
lipping the crumbling ledges of my mind.

The innumerable rustles of existence
swelling visibly between the clock's death rattle
tenacious fingers of earth
pushing up through jagged pores of concrete
defying the crushing feet of men
in singsong streets of old blind houses.
Affinity glimmering briefly, beautifully
in known never-known faces of singular strangers
in broken burning alleys of sunset.
The electric hum of creation
caught once in the satin swish
of a girl's airy dress
down an unremembered avenue.
The bleak blanched limbs of winter
mirrored in green-weeded waters.
A voice babbling in an empty room
to drown its own dull rebellion
hemmed in by an iron heritage

of blackened chimney stacks and gaseous buses
and uncharted backyards bilge-bulging with unfed cats.

A hovel of rust-shining squalor
heaped against the sky
small impetuous beasts embroiled with love and lust
holy novenas and adultery
rabid publicans in soiled smocks
tolling out the daily ending
yellowing leaves of books
shadowed in lickspittle corners.
A hand lightly on my sleeve
and the loneliness of being on earth.

Frostbite

I might have made a poem of this
a month, a year, a decade ago,
the bleak and broken-back garden,
the trees that died in infancy.

Now there is nothing to write about
in a morning big with thunder
and rain lashing my low wooden roof.
The savage and tender green
of the bruised grass outside my window,
the wind suddenly dying
at the far end of a cloud.
Hungry cats arched crooked over garbage bins.
The rainy smell of upturned earth
and birds falling instantly silent
down jagged steppes of sky.

I might have made a poem of this
when I was young, not long ago.
Some familiar addition
some fine fierce frenzy for life
could have made this a rounded number,
could have made this music.

Now I need only remember
this shadow falling on summer
and the silence of another
above the purple roar of thunder.

Spring

Above the reek of turpentine and linseed oil
and cabbage odors trailing from the kitchen
Spring assails my senses
and giddies my heart long schooled in winter.

Sparrows for the working man
set up a turmoil in the stunted bushes
and an out-of-bounds blackbird lords the sky
above the television spires.

I know spring is come home
not by sight of leaf or sound of bird
but that my heart wakes from solitude
and leaps out of anguish to meet her.

My Ship

When I was a lad my bed was the ship
that voyaged me far through the star-dusted night
to lands forever beyond the world's lip
dark burning olive lands of delight
across blood-red oceans under the stars
lorded by the scarlet splendor of Mars.

And always the night was loud with the roar
of flame-nostriled horses flying over the waves
bearing great urns of nectar to a diamonded shore
to madden fat kings and despoil obsequient slaves.
And high over the enchanted orb of my eye
bright galleons of singing men passed in the sky.

And they sang of strange things all glory and fire
of water turning to wine and men rising from dead
and I trembled with a wild and fearful desire
at things that filled me with such joy and such dread.
And their songs filled the hidden places of my heart
till part was whole and whole was part.

Climbing to bed in that lost magical time
was ascending to great secret galaxies of truth
where all meaning was couched in one singular rhyme
that would open only to the unwoken beauty of youth.
And my ship was beautiful and strong and clean
sailing to glories by the mere eye unseen.

It is only a bed now spread with eiderdown
and the sheets merciless chains holding me down.

Waking

When you appeared
that ordinary afternoon
over the crumpled brow of the years
I understood only
a slow astonishment.

You came out of October
with strange beginnings in your hands
to one who had not yet had a beginning
and discerned an end in every departure.
I envied the fate of young twenty-less Chatterton
dying his incandescent death
and Keats giving his holy flesh
to Roman worms to make earth nobler.
Fire then was fire to me
love a cold flame
a static echo in the mind
no thrill in the torture
of things unrealized.

You came
and now you whip my heart to life again
with silken whips of pain.

Muted

I suffer from an impediment
of the soul;
I am a deaf-mute
in thought;
the loneliness of another
shouts at me in baffled hurt
across the cosmic widths of a street
above the metallic sirens of traffic
in velvet-plush wastes of lounge bars
pounding with bone-bare knuckles
upon the subtler bars of thought
begging admittance
begging heed
begging to be heard in all that willful wilderness.
And I hear, I heed, I listen
but cannot reply
being mute
for I am without the key to either of our prisons
and the oceanic spaces roll soft and sullen
between our inlocked island souls
tossing our shipwrecked cries wearily into nowhere
and nowhere do we find a quiet shore to walk upon
and quietly discover each other
needless of the empty theater of words;
only the impassioned impeded soul stuttering in its cage
spluttering in its rage
helpless against controls ironclad
raging to be a moment free
eloquent and free as it was meant to be

and ah! the deaf-mute unuttered unutterable thoughts
broken on their brief doomed career
fall limply to earth between us
dead as any leaves in any dead season
and Despair the faithful lapdog
safe on its lonely hill
watches the human dumb show out of old sardonic eyes
waiting to be called home
as called it will be
to the hollowed hearts of men.

Yesterday I saw a lame bird indifferently maimed
hobbling under my window
flapping its shattered wing at the sky
and its eloquence stopped my breath.

The Lost Prize

My soul was drunk, but my mind quick
with daggered hints of truth
    the dumb rhetoric
of the unseen play behind curtained lids.
        I was sick
with stale porter and the staler dreams
      that squirmed and whimpered
in my tangled guts. Voices that held no sound
      flushed faces that simpered
in imbecilic pay-night bliss.
     Port and sherry mouths someone wanted to kiss.
Men singing In Dublin's Fair City with pipes of clay
    stuck grim in toothless gaps
     brown beer from taps
cascading into tilted tumblers;
    shawled women with puckered eyes
     and flat withered paps
whispering blasphemies in luscious asides
    soft as spider's spinning
      sharp as upthrust swords
a leaping Etna spray of words
    in the blue tobacco air
      swirling to the oak beams
        undiscovered underground seams
of burnt-out undreamt-of dreams
    crammed sweat-stuck in stall-like snugs
      as cattle on market day.

And surprisingly you came
emptied quite of praise or blame
          deep and cool as a Sunday pool
               a stillness in chiffon and lace
a pause in a mad inner dialogue of garbled eloquence
          remote, refined out of existence
a pale shimmer of knee under your dress
          a half-opened volume
               your semi-smile solemn
a pint of black porter between me and that improbable heaven
               under your dark level brows.

Voices crackled on
static in the humming ether
          a backroom barroom bedlam raucous and loud
inhuman cadences
          falling through a purple cloud
drip-drip-dropping into my bruised mind
          a lair of jungle beasts splendid and blind
blithe and brave in their doomed dust
          and useless shining warrior rust;
no behindness
          no quick of elemental lust
beyond the fatuous stare
          the drooling tender obscenities
               the gnarled ever-reaching fingers.

And you my Barrett-Browning, folded hands in lap
      a slow star across a moveless tide
a deathless dream that had already died
      so far beyond my stunted life
a flowering tree lightning-cut.
      I stared dully at a vein in your foot.

Eureka Etcetera

All this quite unremarkable day
the livelong lifeless hours
I chased my thoughts over the mental fields
mice in the corn
rats in the cellar
bats in the battered belfry
up and down the niggling nooks and cantankerous crannies
hunting the apt phrase
groping for the apposite term
hoping for the ultimate in spleen
with you minnow-like stuck in the glue of mind-matter
spurring on my spite to horrific horizons
in hopeful vengeful quest of electric eloquence;
you the very star I once sailed under
the stake at which my life burned bright
now owlishly beyond my frail strangleholds
ripping asunder my little lucid universe
with thunder of sagacious silence;
and nowhere could I find the holy words
nowhere the fiery fulminations of poetic wrath
that would unscrew my scalded soul
and shower forth from my improbable Parnassus
the lava of my erupting ego
the coals of glowing indignation;
so all this unremarkable day
all the livelong lifeless hours
I toiled mightily as any Greek sage
in pursuit of Jupiter's thunder
till wrath itself coiled up and slumbered
ensnared in its own shackles.

Then of a sweet stupendous sudden
I found the way
knew what to say
and with satanic relief could have cried;
my dear
I could not love you *less* if I tried.

City Cameo

A quayside hovel, a tenement slum
unlikely place for Cupid to come.
And my Molly standing at the door
looks very much like a halfcrown whore.

Yet I will love my woman till Judgment Day
and keep what the dustmen can't cart away.

Possession

You, who know not wisely but too well,
                must not imagine my life single, dry,
a mirrored half-smile contemplating itself, narcissus-held;
                for under my polar-opposite star
one image fills the eye

                of my world for its joy,
one bodkin stabs the flesh that is likewise the spirit
                for its awakening, to quicken with the sensitive will
the recluse soul and keep always in the pitiless gaze

                and glare of praise one princedom stark in lucid air
and islanded; so striving to attain, I gain a gift of you
                priceless in the closed commerce of mind a bargain rar

beyond knowing; for you are all lavish and flare of delight
                that stings the incumbent soul to ecstasies of zealous pa
and I, though I have you not, have you yet more fine
                in the blue intricacies of joy
than here within the mute burden of limbs.

End

Dying is a curious thing.
Not that I have ever quite died
except briefly now and then
in a hot-headed poetic way.
There is nothing ingenious about it.
A quick dolphin-plunge
under black water
and after the first year of mourning
the daisies not undisturbed on your grave.
I could die today with a little effort
with a well-sprung wish I could die today
quietly laughing or crying
without trumpets
without ceremony
without drawing conclusions
in Mount Jerome under the fine wet grass.

Brendan

He roared with that deepbellied growl of sad hilarity
    his gorgon's head and cherub's face
        swimming into view over the pint tops,
and opposite me in the bleak bar he chewed deserted gums,
    mouthing parables and paradoxes and pure plenitudes of pleasure
        in the living thunder of the moment,
the gargantuan gargler of our day with schoolboy mien.

The hallowed profanities hung in the air as incense,
    as so many Halley's comets flaming in the ether of ordinary day;
        his face swam in the smoke, a melancholy moon
in an evening sky of set stars and early rainclouds,
    a warrior of words on the last battlefield,
        toothless, untamed, untimid yet, raising the flag,
tramping toward his unmapped Timbuctoo with tired truculence.

And to the literary den in Hawkins Street we adjourned,
    his blackrobed blackbird of a mother in proud awe
        and myself sweetly crooked in the wheelchair;
he pulverized Luther and Brian Boru
    and long-dead Conn of the hundred heroic orgies
        and spoke with gentle garrulous Godspeed
of that decent, decadent man, the Parisian Joyce
    forever ours, in his dark watchtower on the Seine
        going blind with exile at the fag-end of his days;
a consummation he too devoutly wished,
    to be sent up in righteous flames on the Quays
        by the naïve natives timorous of dying unabsolved
of their literary lusts lying dark on their little lost souls.

The harlequin of every hooley, the wonder of every wake,
    the observed of all observers, the curse of the fair state,
        shaggyheaded Pan with a song for the unbeautiful,
crowned and drowned King Puck clowning for the populace
    ribbing the ribs of the rigid righteous
        with his rash panacea of ribald rhetoric,
anointing our maimed memories with salt.

He, like another, went none too gently into that night
    from whose bourne he will always return tongue in pudgy cheek,
        a rakish refugee from life's dull fanfare
peering into snugs in sad haunt of the chiding citizens he loved
        in whose cause he labored lustily and long;
the cause of the Slate, the Beano, the Uncles,
    the bacchanalian bludgeoning of bloated John Bull,
        Moore Street dealers and the singing pubs
and the holy veneration of Liffey water.

A Glasnevin warbler was singing after hours;
    I toed the new clay on that yellow grave of laughter
        pensive in the perennial pursuit of a pint,
and him beyond the need of it and the pale panegyrics of men.

A Kind of Lament for Patrick Kavanagh

And are you gone on the whisky-wild wind
to help push up eternal demented daisies
and count your bellyful of bruised blessings
in some fool-forsaken furrow of sky?

Out of the rancorous northland you came
on a high wind of bombast
to teach us our poetical manners
surly surgeon with sure steady scalpel
slicing through our parsimonious paeans
brushing hot crumbs off your felicitous fingers
for the rabblement to savor and savage
hawk's face flaming under black sombrero
striding with shoes untied through singing streets
of a lost city that never called you son.

Many's the brash young bard wilted
under the salty slash of your tongue
(myself included
though those were my beardless years)
scowling and growling in your cups
O monarch and messiah of McDaid's
pulverizing the whelping young pups
licking your uncompromising country boots
falling into venomous daydreams
on the national television network.

Were you magnanimous?
Only as Swift was

your gleaming pince-nez in shadow
glittering into our stuttering souls
even on a rare day suffering fools
who put whisky in expecting wisdom to come out
tramping quiet canal banks hands behind back
stopping to be a child again with children
emptying the gems of your unhoarded treasure
under that dense derogatory sky.

On the contrary side of the moon
I heard the wind of your passing
and that night saw a shooting star
and called it mere coincidence.

To Helen Keller

I heard it on a plain undreaming day
hunched by the squat old toadstool of a radio
that never did give out the news clearly anyway.
You had just died.

The house lay in Sunday morning silence.
Out in the dull pavement-gray day
people sulked or strutted to church
full of their little unholy terrors and persecutions.
I nursed my headful of dreary dissipation
half hearing the erratic static of the gut-twisted radio
that remote disembodied faraway stilted voice
jerking over the crammed and jammed airlanes of
                                        man-made mayhem:
"We regret to announce the death of . . ."

I heard the news alone.
Alone when I most needed someone to share this sorrow
and yet would most certainly have resented that intrusion.
Such a sorrow is never shared
as that kind of triumph is seldom won.
I felt a momentary surprise.
Surprise that so beautiful a life should have a closing
so like any other.
As if beauty can ever know a close.

Yet I knew
and felt envious.
Envious of your life and your dying.

A symphony only you could listen to
throbbing at your fingertips like light.
A vision beyond the crazy charade of sight.
A dream torn from pain
that had in it all the music of all the birds
that ever sang in this deaf-mute world.

You who saw such splendor of light
heard such a marvel of music
conversed and had your being with such beauty.
You shrank my shrill little world to an atom
made me lift my eyes to pain
and not decline the chalice.

For My Mother

Only in your dying, Lady, could I offer you a poem.

So uncommonly quiet you lay in our grieving midst
        your flock of bereaved wild geese
pinioned by the pomp and paraphernalia of death
        for once upon a rare time wordless
beyond the raw useless grief of your nine fine sons
        the quiet weeping of your four mantillaed daughters
gathered in desperate amity around your calm requiem hour
        and almost I saw you smile in happy disbelief
from the better side of the grave.

Only in your dying, Lady, could I offer you a poem.

Never in life could I capture that free live spirit of girl
        in the torn and tattered net of my words.
Your life was a bruised flower
        burning on an ash-heap
strong and sure on the debris of your broken decades
        unwilting under a hail of mind-twisted fate
under the blind-fisted blows of enraged love
        turning ever toward the sun of a tomorrow
you alone perceived beyond present pain.

Only in your dying, Lady, could I offer you a poem.

You were a song inside my skin
        a sudden sunburst of defiant laughter

spilling over the night-gloom of my half awakenings
             a firefly of far splendid light
dancing in the dim catacombs of my brain.
             Light of foot and quick of eye for pain
you printed patterns of much joy upon the bare walls of my life
             with broad bold strokes of your Irish wit
flaming from the ruins of your towers.

             Only in your dying, Lady, could I offer you a poem.

With gay uplifted finger you beckoned
             and faltering I followed you down paths
I would not otherwise have known or dared
             limping after you up that secret mountain
where you sang without need of voice or words.
             I touched briefly the torch you held out
and bled pricked by a thorn from the black deep rose of your courage.
             From the gutter of my defeated dreams
you pulled me to heights almost your own.

             Only in your dying, Lady, could I offer you a poem.

I do not grieve for you
             in your little square plot of indiscriminate clay
for now shall you truly dance.

O great heart
             O best of all my songs
                          the dust be merciful upon your holy bones.

A Better than Death Wish

Let me not go tamely out to sea
the eternal sea
the only sea
that waves us on to oblivion.

O let me rant and roar as the very waves
as always down all the bruised days of my reckoning.
Let me shout and scream and laugh and curse
and pray in the hollow rock of my penitence.

Christ, you all-seeing son of an inconceivable woman,
don't let me die between the sheets
or even between the thighs of some foolish ready woman.
Let me die with the wild wind in my few hairs
the mad Irish weather scudding over my mind
the bitter-sweet aftertaste of oaken beer
anointing my senses.

O Lord of wine and water
fire and snow
purifier and destroyer of all my days
grant me this:
That when I die
it will be under an Irish sky.